D0569288

Dedicated to those who believe that with a little faith in themselves, they can reach their hopes and dreams.

© 2007 Bruce Blitz

All rights reserved under the Pan-American and International Copyright Conventions
Printed in China

This book may not be reproduced in whole or in part, in any form or by any means, electronic or mechanical, including photocopying, recording, or y any information storage and retrieval system now known or hereafter invented, without written permission from the publisher.

9 8 7 6 5 4 3 2 1
Digit on the right indicates the number of this printing
Library of Congress Control Number: 2006940115

ISBN-13: 0-978-0-7624-2864-9
ISBN-10: 0-7624-2864-3

Cover design by: Russell Benfanti and Matthew Goodman
Interior design by: Matthew Goodman
Edited by: Kelli Chipponeri

Typography: Meanwhile, Chowerder Head, Futura

This book may be ordered by mail from the publisher. Please include $2.50 for postage and handling.
But try your bookstore first!

Running Press Book Publishers
2300 Chestnut Street
Philadelphia, PA 19103-4371

Visit us on the web!
www.runningpress.com

TABLE OF CONTENTS

WELCOME

HI, I'M BRUCE BLITZ, AND WELCOME TO MY DVD CARTOONING BASICS. IN THIS CASE DVD STANDS FOR DYNAMITE VIDEO DRAWING. WE'RE GOING TO LEARN TO DRAW CARTOONS FROM THE BEGINNING. WE'LL TAKE IT STEP BY STEP AND SOON YOU'LL BE TAKING SIMPLE SHAPES AND TURNING THEM INTO FINISHED CARTOONS. SO GET READY TO EXPRESS YOURSELF AND IMPRESS YOURSELF!

Cartooning
Basics
with
Bruce Blitz

WHAT IS A CARTOON?

WELL, A CARTOON HAS BEEN CALLED AN ABBREVIATED FORM OF ART. WHILE IT'S TRUE THAT YOU CAN CREATE A SIMPLE DRAWING OF A GUY FIXING HIS LEAKY PIPES USING LESS LINES THAN OTHER FORMS OF ART, A CARTOON SHOULD DO MORE.

A CARTOON SHOULD EXPRESS A FUNNY IDEA.

Why do we see cartoons everywhere?
We see cartoons so much because they can
really attract our attention.

WE SEE THEM IN PRODUCTS—LIKE THIS LION,
WHO REPRESENTS A BRAND OF CEREAL.

OR IN ADVERTISING—LIKE THIS
ROADSIDE BILLBOARD.

CARTOONS ARE USED A LOT IN GREETING CARDS,

COMIC STRIPS,

AND ANIMATION.

THAT'S RIGHT, CARTOONS
ARE EVERYWHERE, AND IT'S
UP TO CARTOONISTS LIKE YOU
AND I TO KEEP IT THAT WAY.

Before we begin, I'd like to give you some suggestions on the best way to get the most out of learning with a DVD. Here are some suggestions if it seems like I am going too fast at times.

USE YOUR PAUSE BUTTON SO THAT YOU CAN CATCH UP.

USE YOUR REWIND BUTTON TO WATCH THE SEGMENT OVER AND OVER AGAIN UNTIL YOU FEEL THAT YOU'VE GOT IT!

IT TICKLES! HA HA

USE THE MENU BUTTONS A THE BEGINNING OF THE DVD TO ZERO IN ON THE EXACT SEGMENT THAT YOU WANT TO LEARN.

AND ALWAYS REMEMBER THE FIRST RULE OF CARTOONING... JUST HAVE FUN WITH IT! SO ARE YOU READY? LET'S DRAW CARTOONS!

CARTOON RULES BY BLITZ

ART SUPPLIES

WHEN IT COMES TO ART SUPPLIES, I'VE GOT SOME GREAT
NEWS FOR YOU. YOU'RE NOT GOING TO NEED MUCH.

All you'll need is :

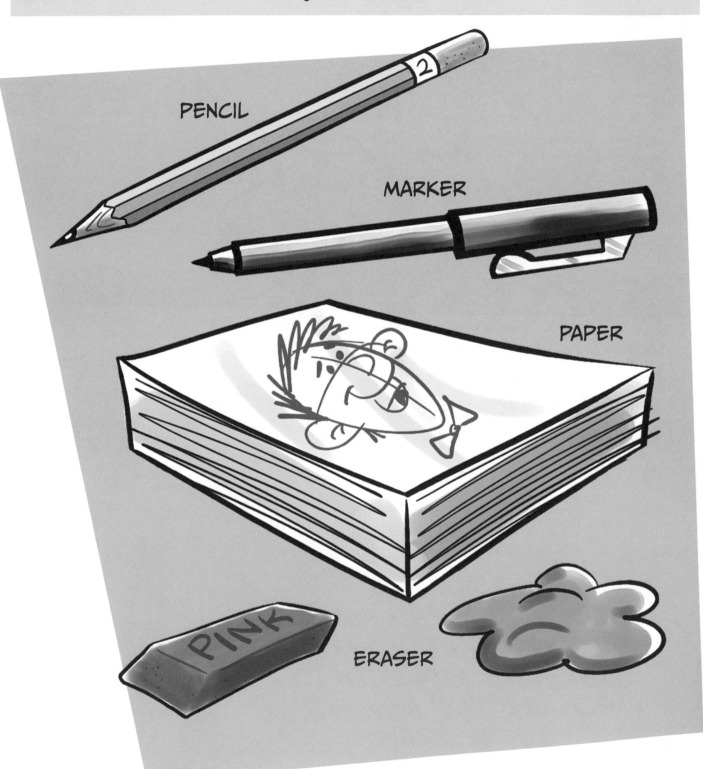

PENCIL

MARKER

PAPER

PINK

ERASER

FIRST, YOU'RE GOING TO USE A LOT OF PAPER WHILE LEARNING, SO I SUGGEST THAT YOU BUY A REAM OF PLAIN OLD COPY PAPER THAT YOU'D USE FOR YOUR COMPUTER'S PRINTER. A REAM IS 500 SHEETS, MEASURES 8-1/2 X 11, RELATIVELY INEXPENSIVE, AND WILL WORK GREAT FOR YOUR CARTOONS.

NEXT, A #2 PENCIL THAT WE USE EVERY DAY WILL WORK GREAT FOR SKETCHING AND LAYING OUT YOUR CARTOONS. DURING THE PENCIL STAGE YOU CAN DRAW IN YOUR GUIDELINES AND ERASE YOUR MISTAKES.

THIRD, THERE ARE MANY DIFFERENT MARKERS THAT YOU CAN BUY. I SUGGEST THAT YOU USE ONE WITH A POINTED TIP SO YOU CAN GET A NICE THICK AND THIN LINE TO YOUR STROKE BY ADDING A LITTLE BIT OF HAND PRESSURE, WHICH ADDS A LITTLE MORE INTEREST TO YOUR DRAWINGS.

FINALLY, YOU SHOULD HAVE AN ERASER. YOU CAN USE A PINK ERASER WHICH IS AVAILABLE ANYWHERE, EVEN ON THE OTHER END OF MOST PENCILS

OR YOU CAN USE SOMETHING A BIT MORE PROFESSIONAL, LIKE THIS KNEADED RUBBER ERASER. IT'S CALLED THAT BECAUSE YOU KNEAD IT LIKE A PIECE OF DOUGH OR CLAY. AND WHEN YOU DO THAT, IT CLEANS ITSELF. IT CAN ALSO BE SHAPED INTO A POINT SO THAT YOU CAN ERASE IN A HARD TO REACH PLACE. KNEADED ERASERS DON'T LEAVE A LOT OF MESSY CRUMBS, WHICH MEANS YOU DON'T HAVE TO KEEP BRUSH-ING THEM AWAY RISKING SMEARING YOUR DRAWING.

All right, that's all you'll need to get started drawing your wacky cartoons. Later on you can check out all of the other neat art supplies that there are available at art and crafts stores. I'll show you how to use these basic tools in our next chapter Cartoon Heads.

CARTOON HEADS

CARTOON HEADS ARE EASY TO DRAW WHEN YOU TAKE THEM STEP BY STEP, AND THAT'S JUST WHAT WE'RE GOING TO DO.

1. We're going to start with a shape, and it's going to be an oval. Draw this shape by holding the pencil and loosely moving your hand around the page until your happy with that motion. Then lower the point to the page. You don't want to start drawing by gripping the pencil real tight and squeaking through three pieces of paper at the same time.

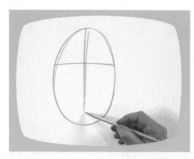

2. We're going to put in some guidelines, which will tell us where to place the features and which direction the character is facing. Draw one horizontally and one vertically in the middle of the oval, which tells us that this character is facing front.

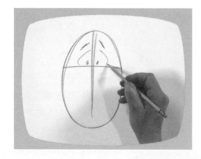

3. Use the pencil to layout all the features. Let's put some dots for eyes, and lines around those dots for the white part of the eyes, and some eyebrows facing up.

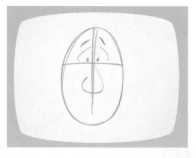

4. Place your pencil right where those guidelines cross and draw a nose.

5. Draw the mouth and wiggle the line a little bit to make it a little more humorous.

6. Draw an ear on each side.

7. Strokes for the hair should be drawn in the same way as we drew the opening shape—loosely so that you get a spontaneous look to your work.

8. Let's switch to the marker. Go back over the pencil lines and make one clean definite line. By varying your hand pressure, you'll get the marker lines to be thick and thin, which adds more interest to your cartoons. This will also get them to look more professional! Sometimes, you have to decide which pencil line to go over with your marker, as during the pencil stage the strokes might have been a bit sketchy.

9. Use your eraser to go over the entire drawing. And you see, the pencil lines leave and the ink lines stay.

10. There you have it... your finished cartoon.

11

This time we're going to start with a different shape and draw a woman.

1. Start with a teardrop shape.

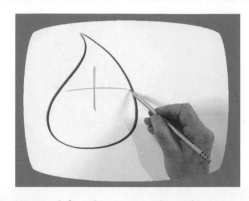

2. Use pencil for the vertical and horizontal guidelines.

3. Go right to marker, if you feel comfortable, to draw her eyes and eyebrows.

4. Where the guidelines cross, draw the letter V on its side for her nose.

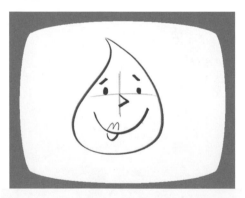

5. Draw a big smile and put in her lips. You can draw the lips a little bit off to the side because everything doesn't have to be perfectly symmetrical and helps to "cartoonify" the face.

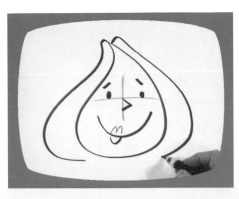

6. Now we'll draw her hair. Place the marker right on top of the teardrop shape and come down to her chin on both sides of her face.

7. When you're drawing cartoon hair, you don't have to draw each strand. You just have to put a few lines next to each other here and there. This will suggest the direction of the hair. Add a couple of strokes for bangs, too.

8. Draw her neck and add some circles to create a necklace.

9. Let's erase the guidelines.

10. Add a little color to this sketch. You can use color pencils, chalks (like I'm using), crayons, or markers. Each method produces a different effect—It is up to you! After all this is your cartoon world.

Look, from a teardrop shape to the finished sketch of a woman.

Let's begin with a football shape to create a really cool character.

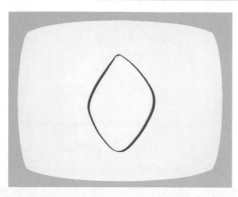

1. Draw a football shape like this.

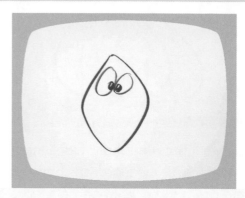

2. Draw 2 ovals for the shape of the eyes and vary their sizes. Now draw the eyes. By drawing them uneven and close together, it makes your character look a little zanier.

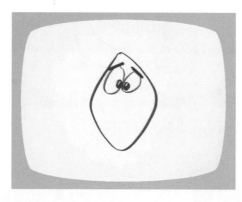

3. Add the eyebrows.

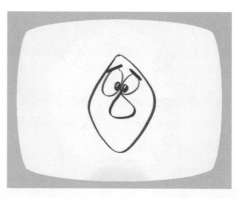

4. Draw a teardrop shape for this guy's nose.

5. Draw an irregular line for a mouth. Now he's coming together!

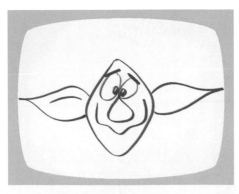

6. Let's give him 2 pointed ears. As you can see, he is turning out to be an alien, so watch out!

7. Draw a few alien freckles on him by adding circles. Also, draw a larger circle around his head so it looks like he's wearing a helmet. (He has to breathe, too!)

8. Aren't all people from other planets green?

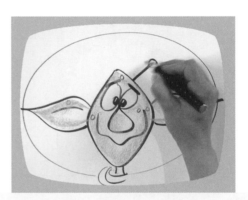

9. We can't forget his antennae.

10. Cartoons don't have to be human, you know!

Different shapes . . . different people!

WHEN YOU CONSIDER ALL OF THE DIFFERENT SHAPES THAT YOU CAN START WITH . . .

. . . VARYING THE FEATURES AND GUIDELINES . . .

. . . AND DON'T FORGET HAIRSTYLES . . .

. . . YOU REALIZE HOW MANY DIFFERENT CHARACTERS YOU CAN CREATE!

TURNING CARTOON HEADS

CARTOON HEADS DON'T ALWAYS HAVE TO BE FACING FRONT.
SOMETIMES THEY NEED TO FACE IN DIFFERENT DIRECTIONS AND
THEY HAVE TO TURN THEIR HEADS. IT MAKES YOUR CHARACTERS
APPEAR MORE LIFELIKE AND NOT WOODEN.

HOW DO WE DO THAT? FIRST IS TO THINK OF THE SHAPE. THAT WE START WITH AS A:

BALLOON

LEFT

RIGHT

AN EGG,

DOWN

UP

A TOMATO,

THE MOON,

OR ANY 3 DIMENSIONAL OBJECT. THIS WAY, WE CAN WRAP THE GUIDELINES "AROUND"
THE SHAPE. WE CAN'T JUST THINK OF THAT SHAPE ON THE PAGE AS A FLAT TWO-DIMENSIONAL
SHAPE. THAT'S HOW YOU GET CARTOON HEADS TO FACE IN DIFFERENT DIRECTIONS.

WRONG

RIGHT

Practice wrapping guidelines around every day objects.
This will help you help add depth to your drawings.

FOOTBALL

BANANA

I'M A-PEAL-ING

NOT AGAIN!

BOWLING BALL & FRIEND

WATT?

LIGHT BULB

Model Sheets—Model sheets are used in animation.
They enable the animator to draw the character in any pose
and what the character would look like facing in any
direction. Check out Hero Guy's model sheet!

HERO GUY

FACIAL EXPRESSIONS

THE CHARACTERS YOU CREATE ARE YOUR ACTORS. THEIR FACES MUST REFLECT WHAT HE OR SHE (OR ALIENS) ARE THINKING OR FEELING. ARE THEY HAPPY, SAD, SCARED, OR WORRIED? YOUR CHARACTERS CAN'T ALWAYS BE SMILING. TAKE A LOOK AT THIS GUY. WHICH FACIAL EXPRESSION WORKS BEST?

NOW HE'S ACTING!

NOW I WOULD LIKE TO INTRODUCE TO YOU SOMETHING CALLED "CARTOON EFFECTS & ACCESSORIES," ALSO KNOWN AS A "CARTOON BAG OF TRICKS!" THEY ARE THOSE LITTLE EXTRA DOODLES AROUND THE DRAWING. THEY ARE VERY IMPORTANT FOR ADDING EXTRA PUNCH TO YOUR DRAWINGS AND HELP YOU TO COMMUNICATE YOUR IDEAS. SUCH AS THE DOTTED LINE COMING FROM THE CHARACTER'S EYES ON PAGE 20, THE PERSPIRATION FROM THE CHARACTER YELLING "LOOKOUT" AND THE TEARDROPS FROM THE SAD GUY.

Cartoon Effects & Accessories

Here we have an example of how changing the "Cartoon Effects & Accessories" alters what the character appears to be doing or thinking.

The lines radiating from this woman makes her appear to be proud!

The Z's coming from this woman makes her appear to be sleeping!

Let's begin by drawing a guy who is scared. I call this sketch "a bunch of circles"—9 of them to be exact!

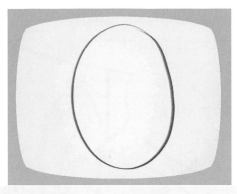

1. Let's count them off by starting with the first large oval, which will be for his head.

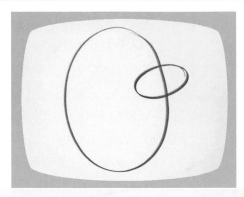

2. Draw an oval for his nose, which will be circle number 2.

3. Make 2 circles for the whites of his eyes (we're up to 4 circles).

4. Draw a large oval for his wide-open mouth with a smaller circle inside for his tongue, which brings us to number 6.

5. A circle on the left side of the opening shape will do nicely for his ear (number 7).

6. Draw 2 small black circles for his eyes, and leave a little white to give the illusion of a highlight (numbers 8 and 9). Also, add his eyebrows and a nostril for some detail on his nose.

7. Now that you've drawn these 9 circles you have got the foundation for a great cartoon sketch. Let's add two lines inside his mouth for his teeth.

8. Draw 3 lines on the top and bottom for the individual teeth.

9. Fill the inside of his mouth with black and add a curved line on the tongue for detail.

10. This next step is what adds the extra humor to this sketch. Draw a fluffy shape for this guy's hair. It has flown off his head!

11. "Cartoon Effects & Accessories," are what will bring this drawing to life. Add some "speed lines" to his hair, so it doesn't' look like it's just floating in the air, perspiration to his face, vibrations to his eyeballs, a caption to show he's screaming, and draw his shoulders and bowtie.

12. Use a little red for his tongue, cheek, and lines radiating from him to bring out the whole drawing. This guy is in TROUBLE!!

This expression will be of a woman who is suspicious of someone.

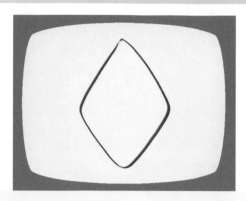

1. We'll start with a diamond shape.

2. When drawing facial expressions, you have to think these actions through. Ask yourself, how would you act if you were suspicious of someone. You might be peeking out of the corners of your eyes, checking them out with one eyebrow up and one eyebrow down, and not quite smiling but not quite frowning.

3. Draw her hair about midway down the opening shape.

4. Next, draw a cloud shape for her curly hair. Add 2 ears and small circles for her earrings.

5. Draw a few lines for a neck and collar.

6. Add some "Cartoon Effects & Accessories," which always help to get your point across to the reader. Include dashes from her eyes to show she is definitely looking at something, curved lines illustrate that she might have turned quickly to look, and a thought balloon showing what she is thinking.

A character laughing hysterically can come in very handy for a cartoon scene!

1. Draw a long skinny oval with your pencil. This is going to be a side view

2. Switching to a marker, draw a big comical nose. His upper lip and mouth are smiling.

3. Complete the rest of his smiling mouth by taking up most of the oval that we started with and draw his chin and neck.

4. Next, draw this fellow's ear. Let's give him some spiky hair on top with a few dots on the side of his head indicating short hair.

5. Drawing his eye as an upside-down V suggests that his eyes are shut tightly. Also, draw his eyebrow facing upward. Now, erase the pencil lines.

6. Let's give this guy some teeth and because he is a zany looking character we will exaggerate them a bit.

7. Drawing his tongue sticking out adds an extra element of humor, too.

8. Now for the "Cartoon Effects & Accessories." Tears of joy, lines showing his head is shaking, and of course, Ha's finish this sketch off nicely!

25

By using 2 or more characters together with the appropriate facial expression, you can create a cartoon scene!

BY ADDING FACIAL EXPRESSIONS YOUR CHARACTERS APPEAR TO BE:

FEELING

ACTING

TO BE...OR NOT TO BE..

THINKING

Blitz Tip — From little thoughts, grow big ideas!

I WONDER WHAT WOULD HAPPEN IF...

HMM..BUT, WHY WOULD...

I'VE GOT IT!

CARTOON TYPES

AS CARTOONISTS, IT'S UP TO US TO CREATE THE RIGHT CARTOON TYPE FOR YOUR CARTOON SCENE. IT'S LIKE CASTING ACTORS FOR A MOVIE OR A PLAY. CARTOON CHARACTERS MUST LOOK LIKE WHO THEY ARE AND WHAT THEY DO. AND WE DO THIS SIMPLY BY ADDING FACIAL ACCESSORIES, LIKE A MUSTACHE, BEARD, HATS, GLASSES, AND MORE.

When you look at these 3 characters you know immediately what type they are:

COWBOY

POLICEMAN

Here is a basic drawing of a guy with just eyes, nose, mouth, and ears, nothing much happening. But let's add some facial accessories to this fellow and we'll turn him into a professor type.

QUEEN

1. First let's give him a distinctive hairstyle. It's floppy almost like a lion's mane.

2. Next, let's put some spectacle type glasses on the end of his nose.

3. Now draw a floppy mustache to match his hairstyle.

4. Draw a figure 8 on its side for a tie. And there you have it—a professor type.

This character could also be a conductor of an orchestra.

This time we'll draw a pirate. We'll start with kind of a husky looking fellow and add facial accessories to him.

1. Let's begin by putting a bandanna on his head with polka dots.

2. Now let's give him some pirate teeth.

3. Draw an earring. That's a facial accessory that will work well.

4. Draw some dots for stubble, like he needs to shave.

5. And what self-respecting pirate wouldn't have a patch? So let's draw him one. There he is . . . "Patch the Pirate"

I don't think this type will work well as a ballerina.

By changing the cartoon effects, clothes, and facial accessories, the same character becomes a different cartoon type!

THIS WOMAN IS A KINDLY GRANDMA TYPE WITH GLASSES.

IF WE ADD FANCY JEWELRY, ROBE, AND OF COURSE, A CROWN SHE BECOMES A QUEEN.

THIS FELLOW IS TIMID AND STUDIOUS WITH LARGE GLASSES AND A BOWTIE.

LET'S CHANGE HIS LARGE GLASSES TO SHADES, GIVE HIM AN EARRING, A HAT, HEADPHONES WITH MUSICAL NOTES, AND HE BECOMES A COOL DUDE!

HEAD WAITER OR A BUTLER

OR A GOURMET CHEF?

 Tip

Practice has no enemies but laziness.

A cartoonist needs to be able to draw a good cartoon baby, so let's do that now in 8 steps.

1. We're going to start with a big circle.

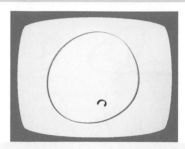

2. When you draw people that are young, like a baby, you want to put the character's features way down low in the shape. We'll start with his nose.

3. Now we'll put a smile right near the bottom of this shape and big full cheeks.

4. Add some eyes and eyebrows.

5. Draw in ears, and he's turning out to be a pretty cute little baby, isn't he?

6. How about a curl right out of the center of his forehead.

7. And we'll draw a bonnet on this fellow, which helps to make this character a baby type.

8. Last, add a lace collar, and there he is—a baby!

Let's turn this average looking guy, who has no facial accessories into an artist.

He has no features that would tell you he is an artist.

Some squiggly lines will work well for this mustache.

Let's draw a "goatee" type beard.

Now, we'll add an artist's beret to finish this creative guy!

Blitz Tip

Cover your refrigerator with lots of drawings!

More Cartoon Types...Yipes!
Look at all the facial props, accessories, and clothing there are on these special characters.

EXECUTIVE

THIS MAN COULD BE A TV BROADCASTER
OR THE CEO OF A COMPANY.

WITCH

THIS WITCH HAS SPECTACLES, STRINGY HAIR,
BAD TEETH, BENT POINTY HAT, AND OF COURSE,
A GREEN COMPLEXION. THE WHITES OF HER
EYES, COLORED IN YELLOW, SQUEEZES OUT
AN EXTRA MEASURE OF HUMOR!

FARMER

HERE IS A FARMER TYPE CHARACTER. HE IS
WEARING A STRAW HAT AND CHEWING ON PIECE
OF WHEAT. HIS BEARD IS ALSO AN IMPORTANT
ELEMENT THAT HELPS TO CONVEY WHO HE IS.

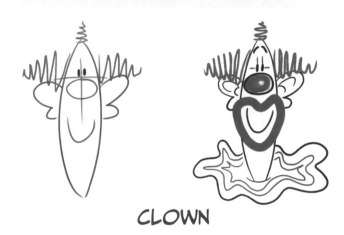

CLOWN

CLOWNS ARE PEOPLE TOO...I THINK!

Let's KID around!

A GIRL WITH EARRINGS
AND SWIMMING GOGGLES
ON HER HEAD.

A BOY WITH BRACES.

A BABY GIRL WITH A PACIFIER AND A
BOW WRAPPED AROUND WHAT LITTLE
HAIR SHE HAS ON HER HEAD!

Different beards and the characters they create! Here are four characters with different types of facial hair and hats.

A PROSPECTOR

SANTA CLAUSE

THE ONLY GOLD THIS GUY HAS EVER FOUND IS IN HIS TOOTH. HIS FACIAL EXPRESSION SHOWS THAT HE IS DOWN ON HIS LUCK. HE IS DRAWN WITH A STRAGGLY BEARD AND MUSTACHE AND HAS AN OLD WORN HAT THAT HE WEARS CROOKED.

HIS BEARD IS DRAWN WITH FLUFFY CURVED LINES LIKE A CLOUD. OF COURSE HE HAS A JOLLY FACIAL EXPRESSION.

A HAPPY GUY?

A SOLDIER FROM THE 1500'S.

THIS GUY HERE CLAIMS THAT HIS BEST FEATURE IS HIS SMILE?

HE HAS A WELL GROOMED BEARD AND MUSTACHE. NOTICE HIS CONFIDENT EXPRESSION.

DIFFERENT TYPE PEOPLE ARE EVERYWHERE, SO DEVELOP THE HABIT OF OBSERVING PEOPLE WHEREVER YOU GO.

CARTOON BODIES

CARTOON BODIES ARE DRAWN MUCH LIKE CARTOON HEADS, BY BUILDING ON SHAPES. WE'LL ADD SOME LINES TO THESE SHAPES, TO MAKE IT EVEN EASIER, AND TURN IT INTO A "STICK FIGURE!"

1. Let's begin by drawing 2 shapes, a circle for the head and rectangle that is a bit wider at the bottom for the torso. Also, use a short line to connect the shapes for the neck.

2. Add a line with an oval for each of this character's legs. The length of these lines will determine the "proportions" of the character, which is up to you!

3. Draw 2 lines for each arm with a small circle for his hands.

4. Use your marker to draw his facial features.

5. Next, draw his shirt by using the pencil lines as a guide. Basically, thicken-up the stick figure.

6. Do the same thing to the arm on the left. His wrist is resting on his hip so his thumb is in the back and isn't visible. Continue using your marker to go over the rest of his shirt and draw one definite clean line.

7. Use your marker to draw his other arm. Next, we'll draw his other hand waving at us. The easiest method I have found for drawing a cartoon hand is to put fingers on a circle. The first question to ask yourself when drawing a hand is which direction is the palm facing? In this case it will be facing us. So, we'll start by putting in his thumb to the left.

8. Let's draw his fingers leaving the center part of the circle open to draw a short curved line for his palm. Cartoon characters, sometimes have three fingers and sometimes they use four. It's up to you.

9. Next, add some "Cartoon Effects & Accessories" around his hand to give the illusion that it's waving. Ink in the legs and shoes, too.

10. Erase the pencil lines and there is your finished character in a basic standing pose.

More about cartoon hands

1. To draw a basic hand, begin with a circle.
2. Add a thumb and fingers to the shape.

Some basic hand positions to practice.

SHAKING HANDS WITH PALMS BOTH WAYS.

PEACE

WAVING

POINTING

HOLDING A BOOK WITH PALM NOT FACING US.

HOLDING AN ICE CREAM CONE (STRAWBERRY) WITH THE PALM FACING US.

37

Let's draw a little girl using more basic shapes.

1. Begin with a circle, triangle, and a rectangle.

2. Draw a couple of ovals for feet and add some lines and shapes for arms. Let's have her holding an ice cream cone.

3. Draw in her facial expression.

4. Notice how the triangle shape becomes her torso wearing a dress.

5. By splitting the rectangle shape in 2, we have this little girl's legs. Just add some detail like her knees, socks, and saddle shoes.

6. See how simple shapes can be used to create cartoon people!

Blitz Tip

If you enjoy what you're drawing, you must be doing it right!

Cartoonists must have a good running pose up his or her sleeve. A running pose shows a character in action. You never know when you'll need it for your cartooning assignment. Also, it's the basis for many action poses.

1. Let's start by drawing a stick figure. The line to the right of the figure is the "Line of Motion". This helps you define the action which in this case is leaning forward.

2. Use your marker, as before, to ink in your sketch. Notice his hair is flowing back as he is running forward.

3. Continue thickening up and defining the shapes and lines. The hand on the right side of this drawing is a clenched fist with the palms facing away from us.

4. Draw his other hand with the palms facing us. Use your marker to thicken up the lines used for his legs so that they look like a pair of pants.

5. Once you have completed inking in your drawing . . .

6. . . . use your eraser to erase your pencil lines!

7. Draw his shadow on the ground by leaving a little space between his foot. This makes him appear to be in the air and going that much faster! By adding "Cartoon Effects & Accessories" like, speed lines, puffs of smoke, dust, and perspiration, this guy looks like he's running off the page!

BODY LANGUAGE!
Let's draw some more cartoon bodies utilizing what we have already learned and add one more important cartooning element to the sketch. Body language is an extension of facial expressions. It further helps to show what a character is thinking or feeling-don't forget to add those "Cartoon Effects & Accessories."

THIS GIRL IS STANDING UP TALL AND LEANING BACK A BIT WITH HER ARMS OUT STRAIGHT, BECAUSE SHE IS HAPPY ABOUT HER NEW PUPPY!

THIS POOR FELLOW WITH HIS CLENCHED FISTS IS VERY FRUSTRATED. HIS BODY LANGUAGE CERTAINLY SHOWS IT! NOTICE HOW HIS HAT FLYING OFF OF HIS HEAD ADDS AN EXTRA ELEMENT OF HUMOR. NOW YOU'RE CARTOONING!!

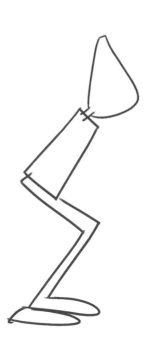
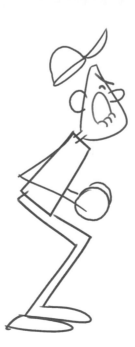

THIS GUY'S BASIC BODY CONSTRUCTION IS BUILT ON WAVY LINES. HE IS VERY SAD BECAUSE HE CAN'T AFFORD TO BUY A NEW TELEVISION. HE IS SLUMPING FORWARD WITH HIS HANDS IN HIS POCKETS WHILE LOOKING OVER HIS SHOULDER. A WELL THOUGHT OUT BODY LANGUAGE POSE CAN TELL A WHOLE STORY!

Blitz Tip

Success is with those who keep trying!

CARTOON ANIMALS

CARTOON ANIMALS ARE AN EXTREMELY POPULAR AREA OF CARTOONING AND ONE OF MY FAVORITE SUBJECTS TO DRAW. THE KEY TO DRAWING THEM IS TO SIMPLIFY THEIR FEATURES.

HERE I HAVE DRAWN A REALISTIC SKETCH OF A GIRAFFE. IN ORDER TO CARTOONIFY HIM, WE SIMPLIFY HIS FEATURES AND KIND OF SMOOTH OUT THE LUMPS AND BUMPS.

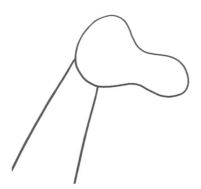

1. Start with a peanut shape for his head and 2 lines for his long neck.

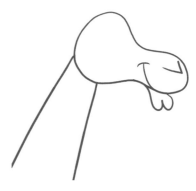

2. Draw a smile, a protruding lower lip, and a V shape nose.

3. Giraffe's have very expressive eyes with long lashes.

4. Their horns are great features for cartooning. They almost look like lolly-pops. Also, accentuate their floppy ears.

5. Next, draw his mane with quick back and fourth strokes and create some irregular shapes on his neck and head.

6. Add some color and there you have a great cartoon giraffe—just by simplifying his features.

Cartoon dogs are a cartoonist's best friend!

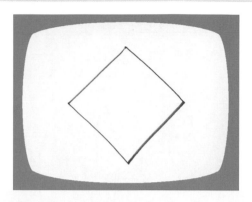

1. Let's start with a diamond shape.

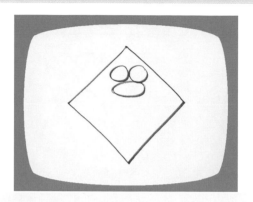

2. Right in the middle of that diamond, we're going to put an oval. That's going to be for his nose. Then draw two circles for his eyes.

3. Add the eyes and eyebrows. Fill in his nose and leave a little white space, which creates a highlight.

4. Now right out of that nose draw a line coming down to make his smile. Add some circles for whiskers and his tongue. Don't forget a few funny looking hairs at the top of his head!

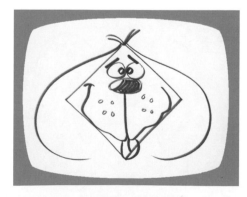

5. This next step really "dogifies" it. Draw 2 floppy ears.

6. Use some brown for his ears and red for his tongue to finish "Doug the Dog."

Have you ever heard it said that people look like their pets or pets look like their people? I don't know which way it is, but we're out to prove that that is definitely true! We're going to draw a parrot and the person who owns this parrot.

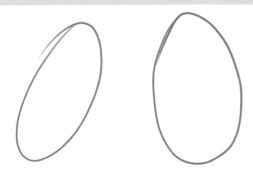

1. Start with 2 ovals.

2. Add a circle on each shape for eyes. Draw a beak for the parrot and a nose for her owner.

3. Draw smiles, eyes and eyebrows.

4. Add feathers and simulate that shape with hair. Don't forget the funny looking curly feather/hair on top.

5. Now add feet and a necklace...

MOLLY WANT A CRACKER...AWK!!

6. And color them in! Meet Polly & Molly!

More People & Pets

DAN AND HIS AFGHAN

BRIAN AND HIS LION

BEN AND
HIS PENGUIN

CHUCK
AND DUCK

45

Blitz Tip

A great way to practice drawing cartoon animals
is to sketch at a zoo, an aquarium, or even right from
books. Remember the key—simplify their features.

INANIMATE OBJECTS

ONE OF THE THINGS THAT I LOVE THE BEST ABOUT DRAWING CARTOONS IS HOW YOU CAN MAKE ANYTHING HAPPEN. YOU CAN EVEN GIVE LIFE TO INANIMATE OBJECTS. WHAT IS AN INANIMATE OBJECT? IT'S AN OBJECT THAT ISN'T ALIVE. BUT WE CAN MAKE THEM LIVE IN CARTOONS.

1. Let's draw a cloud, which is very simple to do. Curved lines like this will create a fluffy shape.

2. It's going to be a storm cloud so we're going to put the appropriate facial expression right in the center. Start with a curved line for a cheek.

3. Draw 2 eyes shut, with the eyebrows facing down, and a nose.

4. A small circle is all that is needed for his mouth.

5. Draw his lower lip under the circle and his other cheek.

6. If he is a busy storm cloud, he'll be busy blowing up a storm, so add the "Cartoon Effect & Accessories" of wind coming from his mouth. Now, we've made this inanimate object come to life by giving him a personality!

Let's draw another inanimate object to bring to life and this time it will be a cell phone.

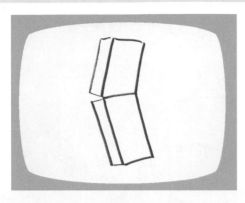

1. Start with two tilted cube shapes. These will the foundation for a cartoon cell phone.

2. Draw 2 arms on the cell phone. You can do this sort of thing in cartooning. Notice the cartoon gloves he's wearing.

3. Draw the screen and some detail for the dial buttons.

4. Now, draw his facial expression, which as you can see he isn't feeling too well!

5. Add some "Cartoon Effects & Accessories" that show he is dizzy.

More inanimate objects coming to life! In order to come up with ideas for a personality to give an inanimate object, just think of what that object does for ideas. What these characters are saying reflects the object's purpose.

A SOUP LADLE

SPHERE

CHICKEN SOUP... MY FAVORITE!

A WATER COOLER

CYLINDER

CUBE

I'VE GOT IT UP TO HERE!

BREAK OBJECTS DOWN TO THEIR BASIC FORMS IN ORDER TO DRAW THEM.

A GUITAR AMPLIFIER

CUBE

TOO LOUD!!

YOU CAN FIND OBJECTS JUST ABOUT ANYWHERE YOU LOOK!

ED ERASER SAYS:

A MISTAKE IS A CHANCE TO TRY AGAIN!

SAVE US FOR A RAINY DAY!

CYLINDER

I'LL NEVER GET ANY SLEEP!

A MUG OF COFFEE

PAPER MONEY

Blitz Tip

SO DRAW AN OBJECT, FIND A PLACE ON IT TO PUT A FACIAL EXPRESSION THAT BEST FITS IT'S PERSONALITY AND YOU'LL HIT A

HOMERUN!

SMACK

49

DOODLE TRICKS

WELCOME TO BLITZ CARTOON DOODLE TRICKS. WHAT ARE CARTOON DOODLE TRICKS? IT'S WHEN YOU TAKE A NUMBER, A LETTER, OR EVEN A WORD, AND TURN IT INTO A FINISHED CARTOON. THE BEST PART ABOUT CARTOON DOODLE TRICKS IS THAT MOST OF THE DRAWING IS DONE SIMPLY BY WRITING THE NUMBER OR THE LETTER.

Sam the Farmer

1. Let's start with the letter S.

2. Draw a circle for an eye. Cut that circle in half, and add the eye looking at us.

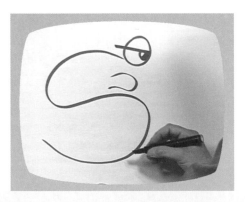

3. This part of the S will be a nose, so let's add a nostril.

4. Draw curved lines for his head and ear and down for his neck.

5. Turn this part of the S into this fellow's beard.

6. Add his smile, hair and S is for Sam the Farmer!

Santa's Favorite REINDEER

1. Start with the number 8.

2. Draw two dots for eyes and eyebrows.

3. Make a circle on this bottom of the 8.

4. Add some floppy ears on each side.

5. Draw in some antlers.

6. I think you can tell who this is, especially when we put a little red on the nose. That's right, the number 8 turned into Santa's favorite reindeer!

If you can write the word duck, guess what, you can draw a duck.

DUCK

1. D-U-C-K—this is going to be a quickie!

2. Put a dot right there for an eye.

3. Close up the K and add a nostril. As you can see, it's turning into a great cartoon duck.

4. Draw some fluffy lines to create feathers.

5. Let's put this little guy in the water.

6. This sound effect shows you that this isn't a quickie, it's a quackie!

BAD BABY

1. This time let's start with a bean shape to draw a baby.

2. Draw 2 ears, 2 eyes, and 2 eyebrows facing downwards, which shows us that this little guy isn't too happy!

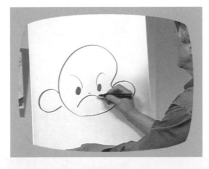

3. Let's draw his mouth frowning with a curved line and a dash for the nose.

4. Draw a big curl right on his forehead and some lines to indicate hair on top of his head.

5. Draw in some more hair around his ears. He is not too happy because he's got his bib on and he doesn't want to eat.

6. So, the question is: What happens to bad babies who won't eat their vegetables?

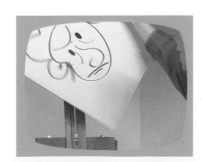

7. By turning this sketch over you'll see, they turn into mean old men!

Here are a few examples of how you
can take a symbol or an object and turn it into
something that pertains to that symbol or object!

AN ACORN TO A SQUIRREL THAT LOVES THEM!

A MUSICAL NOTE TURNS INTO THIS TOOTHY SINGER!

FROM A NOSE THAT SNIFFS TO A BLOODHOUND THAT IS KNOWN FOR THE SAME THING!

55

IN CLOSING . . .

I HOPE YOU HAVE ENJOYED DRAWING ALONG WITH ME. LIKE MUSIC, ART, SPORTS, COMPUTERS, OR ANY OTHER WORTHWHILE GOAL, YOU HAVE TO PRACTICE, AND NEVER QUIT! SUCCESS IS WITH THOSE WHO KEEP TRYING. I'M BRUCE BLITZ SAYING, THANKS FOR BEING WITH ME AND *KEEP ON CARTOONING!*

Cartooning
Basics
with
Bruce Blitz

IF YOU ENJOY
DYNAMITE VIDEO DRAWING™
YOU MAY ENJOY MY OTHER
PRODUCTS AS WELL!

Blitz® Ultimate
Cartooning Kit

Blitz®
Toon-rific™
Craft Kit

Blitz® Mini
Cartooning Kit

Blitz®
Cartooning
Kit

Blitz®
Big Book
of Cartooniing